Honey Bunny says,
"Be happy, be kind."
Lavelle Carlson

Bee, Honey Bunny and Me

Yucky, Yummy Carrots

by

Lavelle Carlson

Illustrated by

John D. Moulton

Bee, Honey Bunny and Me

1st Edition

Written by Lavelle Carlson

Illustrated by John D. Moulton

ISBN: 978-1-7344427-2-4
ISBN10: 1-7344427-2-4

Visit:
SLPStoryTellers.com
&
HoneyBunnysBurrow.com

Acknowledgements

Thanks to my very supportive husband, LeRoy Carlson. Thanks also to my daughters, Liana and Lisa, for sharing their precious children with a grandmother who wants her grands to appreciate the importance of books and the importance of animals and all life. Love to Taya, Niko, Emory, Rhodes, and Leni.

This book was inspired by the author's youngest granddaughter who, at the age of two, became "the bunny whisperer". She loves to play with the bunnies that run in her backyard.

This work would not have been the same without the creative feedback and insight of illustrator, John D. Moulton. His experience as a portraitist added so much emotion to the visual elements of the story.

Both author and illustrator would also like to thank the *Beatrix Potter Society* for acknowledging John's use of *Peter Rabbit* in this story, shown as a battered old poster on the little girl's bedroom wall.

Let me tell you a story

Once upon a time there was a little girl they called, 'The Bunny Whisperer'. She loved the natural world, the trees, the flowers and all the animals too, but most of all she loved her bunnies.

In fact there wasn't much that nature brought her way that Leni didn't like.

But one thing was for sure, for reasons known only to her, Leni simply hated carrots.

Then, one night a baby bunny with that same issue, came to her in a dream. There, she watched from a distance as the baby bunny's mommy found a friend with an answer that would make her baby bunny very happy indeed.

Let's take a look for ourselves and see just how it all came about.

"Mommy, can I be a bunny?"

"Yes, you can be a bunny.
Bunnies love carrots."

"Yucky! I hate carrots!"

"Well, it is time to go to sleep
and dream about bunnies.
I love you, Leni."

"Goodnight, Mommy."

Nibbles, Nasher & Chomp

What can I do to help my bunny eat carrots?

Let's go to
Mrs. Farmer's garden.

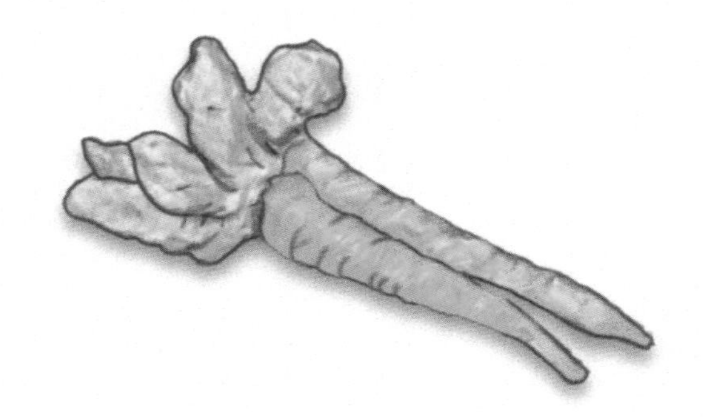

"Look, Baby Bunny!
We have yummy orange carrots.
Carrots help you hop high and fast."

"Yucky, yucky orange carrots!
Yucky, yucky crunchy carrots!
I don't want to eat carrots."

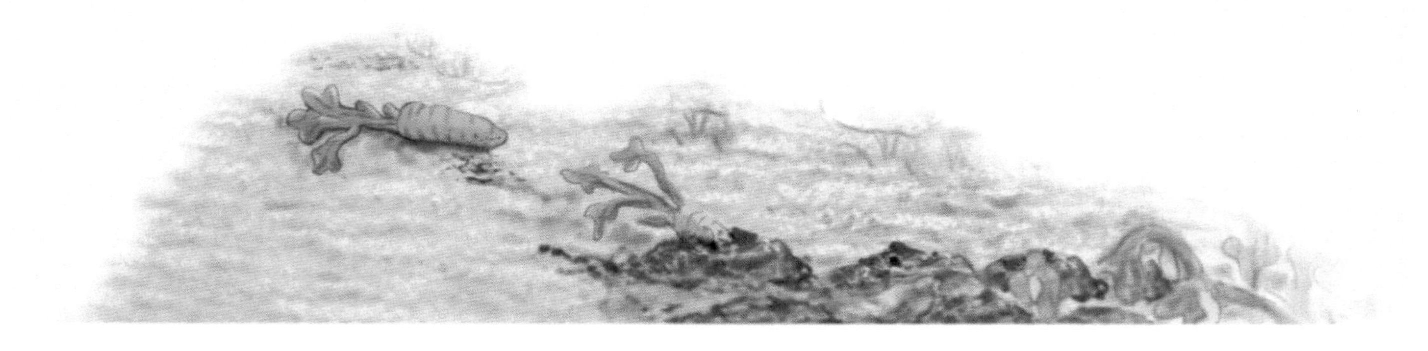

Hi!
My name is
Honey Bunny.
Follow me. You
will see why my
Mommy Bunny
calls me
Honey Bunny.

"Baby Bunny, it's time to eat.
I have something yummy for my
hungry baby bunny."

"Yummy, yummy
in my tummy.

What is it?
Where is it?"

Let's take some yummy honey to help baby bunny enjoy her carrots!

Look, Baby Bunny! The bees are dropping golden honey on the green carrot tops.

Yummy, yummy.
The green carrot tops
taste like honey.

Look! The bees are now putting honey on the orange carrots.
OK, I will try the yucky orange carrots with honey.

Yummy! The orange carrot is not yucky. It is sweet and yummy in my tummy.
Ah, you love honey carrots. You are now my Honey Bunny.

And so it was that Leni and her new dream-time friend, Honey Bunny, learned that sometimes when you don't like good, healthy food, you simply mix it up with something you love, so that you grow big, healthy and strong.

Now, Honey Bunny can enjoy her carrots with cousins, Nibbles, Nasher and Chomp.

The next day, Mommy Bunny took Honey Bunny back to the hive to say thank you once more for their gift.

Let's turn the page and discover what they learned.

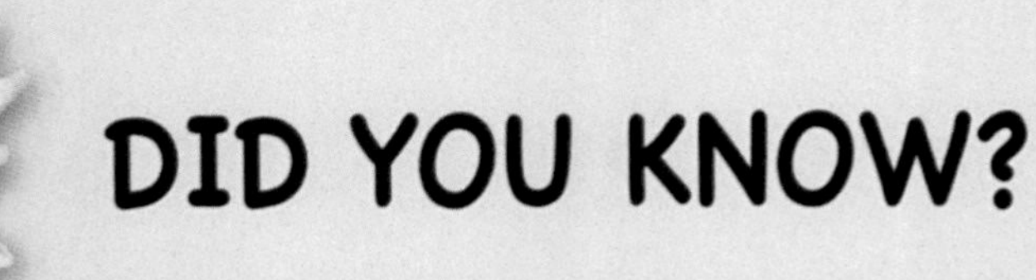

DID YOU KNOW?

Without honey bees all our lives would be very different.

Bees make it possible for fruit trees and many veggies to turn their flowers into fruit.

How?

Well, let's take an apple tree as just one example. Believe it or not every flower, or blossom as we call them, contains a magic dust that we call pollen. For that flower to become an apple, mother nature decided it needs the magic dust from another apple tree to make it happen.

Without bees to help take that magic pollen dust from one tree to another, all those trees would only have the wind to help. That would mean a lot less fruit for you and me to enjoy.

So, when you see a busy bee collecting that magic dust and taking it from one tree to another, remember that he's working for all of us too.

So, leave him to his work and just like Honey Bunny, whisper a thank you for all he does to make sure you can enjoy all your favorite fruits and veggies too.

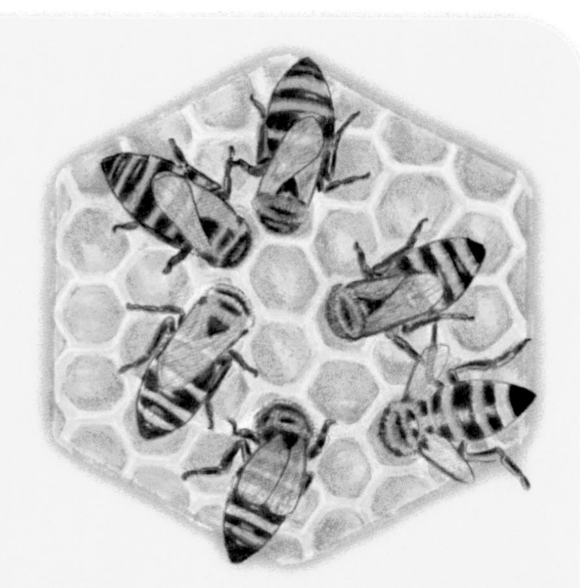

And that's only half the story!

As their thank you to the bees, those fruit trees and many other plants let the bees take lots of that magic pollen dust home to their hive where they use it to help make honey for you and me, and keep a little for themselves, of course.

So let's do everything we can to help those busy bees do their work, making good food happen for you and me.

A NOTE TO PARENTS
(and children too)

Plight of the Bumblebee!

It's great to know our honey bees are thriving well in today's turbulent world. Most are 'domesticated' creatures, cared for by many from farmers to hobby-shop beekeepers all over the world.

But the same is not true for the precious Bumblebee. Though they are not honey-makers, they are prolific pollinators - some say many times more productive than their many cousins out there in the world of bees.

Their lives are short - just one season, and their colonies small, rarely more than two-hundred and fifty strong, unlike their honey bee friends that live for years, often in colonies numbering tens-of-thousands.

Given this, bumblebees suffer great hardship due to the perils of insecticides and even climate change.

To learn more about these invaluable little creatures and how you can help ensure their survival, please visit these great websites.

IN THE USA
Bumblebee Watch:
BumblebeeWatch.org

IN THE UK & EUROPE
Bumblebee Conservation Trust:
BumblebeeConservation.org

I see little birds flying.
What are they doing?
They are bees. Let's take a look.

Bzzz, bzzz. You look sad.
My Baby Bunny will not eat her carrots.
Bzzz. Maybe I can help. I shall return from my hive soon.

For Healthy Humans

Honey Bunny

would like to suggest you try*

Sunny Anderson's

Honey Glazed Carrots

HERE'S THE RECIPE

Ingredients:

Salt
1 pound of baby carrots
2 tablespoons of butter
2 tablespoons of honey
1 tablespoon of lemon juice
Freshly ground black pepper
1/4 cup of chopped flat-leaf parsley

Instructions:

In a medium saucepan, bring water to boil.
Add salt and then carrots and cook until tender 5-6 minutes.
Drain carrots and add back to pan with butter, honey and lemon juice
Cook until a glaze coats the carrots, 5 minutes.
Season with salt and pepper and garnish with parsley

Visit: SunnyAnderson.com for more

*Unsponsored

Made in the USA
Columbia, SC
02 April 2022

58400603R00018